Table of Contents

Providing Options Publishing Company

Understanding the Crisis of the Black Male

*A Handbook On Raising Black Boys To Be
Responsible Black Men*
by
Ajuma Muhammad

ver Photo by "Kuumba" Katrina Butler Powell
ver Design by Elaine P. Young
oto Credits by Maurice Meredith
ok Editing by Geri Mitchell-Robinson
pyright@1999 by Ajuma Muhammad

nted in the United States of America
3N - 0-9648181 - 2 - 4

I.

Foreword

WARNING

Explosive!!!   This book will challenge your present way of thinking and hopefully stimulate you to examine your role in the liberation or destruction of Black males in this society. Are you a part of the conspiracy to destroy Black males?

This product may not be suitable for those patriotic American souls who are blinded by America's attempt to police the world. Side effects include: self-awareness, positive self-worth, self-motivation and cultural enrichment.

The mental consumption of the material in this book may be hazardous to close-minded people. It is highly recommended that you seek the advice of your inner soul before absorbing this material. The author claims no responsibility for the reader who journeys beyond this point in the book.

II.

The Holy Bible

"If my people, which are called by my name, shall humble themselves, and pray, and seek my face, and turn from their wicked ways; then will I hear from heaven, and will forgive their sin, and will heal their land."

II Chronicle
Chapter 7:14

III.

<u>Dedication</u>

To the ancestors for paying the ultimate price with their lives. This ultimate sacrifice has afforded me the opportunity to express myself fully with the words in this book. This book is dedicated to:

My mother, Beatrice Hudson

My father, Wilbert Thomas
and
Step-father Marion Hudson

My lovely wife Ajanna Muhammad, my children Ishmael Muhammad, Danielle Moore, Dawanna Moore,
and Davione Moore

People who have inspired me to become the man I am today

Verge "Sage" Gillam	Joseph Scoggin Jr.
Malik Ahmed	Anthony Shahid
Jawanza Kunjufu	Malcolm X
Naim Akbar	Calvin Perkins
Donald Suggs	Robert L. Williams
Lores Wells	Donald Wells
Betty C. Patton	Patrick Stack
Minister Louis Farrakhan	Hon. Elijah Muhammad
Sultan Muhammad	Dorothy Smith

IV.

Acknowledgments

First, I would like to give thanks and praise to Almighty God Allah who blessed me to overcome a mentally and physically destructive lifestyle. This enabled me to create the Association of African-American Role Models organization in 1986. Your blessings have given me the opportunity to inspire others, and to be an encouragement to other Black males. I am a servant of Your Divine inspiration and I am eternally grateful for Your guidance while writing this book.

I want to give a very special thanks to my editor, Geri Mitchell-Robinson. Thank you for your countless hours of reading, writing, editing, book reviewing, and incredible insight to see this project through to completion. Thank you for your hard work and dedication. This work would not have been possible without your expertise and the support of your family.

Thank you Jamilah El-Amin, author of "*Empowering the Black Woman*" for your direction and encouragement. Thanks for showing me that a project of this magnitude was possible.

Elaine Young, thank you for your patience and continuous effort in making the book's artwork magnificent.

Maurice Meredith, thank you for your vision. Your ability to look through a camera lens, and make art out of life is untouchable.

"Kuumba" Katrina Butler Powell, your work is as creative as you. Thank you for an amazing book cover.

Special thanks to the AAARM students, their families, friends and the role models who volunteer their time weekly to inspire Black youth. I also thank those who have supported AAARM over the years. We pray that we have been instrumental in your lives as well.

Thank you Minister Louis Farrakhan and the Nation of Islam for giving me spiritual enlightenment, self-development and wisdom as taught by the Honorable Elijah Muhammad. It is comforting to know that all things are possible when you submit your will to God's will.

I thank all the members of my family. Thank you mother, Beatrice and stepfather Marion Hudson; Sisters, Donna, Mary, Bernadine and brother Daniel Thomas for your support, and my father Wilbert P. Thomas who's watching over my work in spirit. Thank you for supporting and guiding me throughout my early development. May Allah grant you paradise.

Finally and with the utmost gratitude, I thank my wife Ajanna. Words cannot express how grateful I am to you for being my soul mate and friend. Thank you for your support while I wrote this book. Your patience and grace have granted me the security to know that home is all right when I'm in the "hood" working with the young brothers. You are a Godsend!

I love you all,
Ajuma Muhammad

V.

Tribute to my Wife, Queen and Soulmate

"Ajanna Muhammad"

Day by day, year by year, I love you more and more.

It's more than just your smile and special loving

touch that make you so unique. It's the way you put

so much of yourself into everything you do...

It's more than just

Your thoughtfulness and playful nature

that make you so much fun to be with.

It's the way you make every day more special than

the last...

It's more than just

your passionate heart

and endearing ways

that make me love you like I do.

It's everything you do,

everything you are.

Thanks a million for all of your support.

CHAPTER ONE

"*We must educate ourselves and our children into the power of knowledge which has elevated every people who have sought and used it.*
We must give the benefit of our knowledge to the elevation of our own people."

Hon. Elijah Muhammad

WHY I WROTE THIS BOOK

Why I wrote this book

I have several reasons for writing this book. Most of my experience is based on my life. I am a Black man who grew up during a time when skin color was not the greatest issue, however, I was perceptive enough to recognize that discrimination was alive and well. God has blessed me to overcome the pitfalls through which many Black males suffer. Perhaps this book will inspire, motivate and be an encouragement to other Black males.

Education is key in any society. It is crucial that African Americans become aware of the tools needed to compete in a world that really does not favor them. Many Blacks believe that their ancestors' contributions are enough to garner fairness today, but that's just a fantasy. The struggle is never going to be over.

One of the greatest tragedies for today's African American is his lack of knowledge and interest in his rich history and culture. Perhaps it's not his fault that he wasn't taught the truth about history in school. But what's the excuse now? Blacks are free to go to the libraries and research their history until they get tired. If their children are still being "fed" the falsehoods about Columbus and the first Kings and Queens, then it is our place to challenge the schools and its teachers.

The omitting or limiting of Black achievement in the American school system is "educationally criminal." Western education has literally castrated people of color leaving them ignorant of their cultural achievements and progress throughout the history of the world.

The distortion and reclaiming of the Black man's history has produced a damaged psychological image for him. Blacks now strive to find their rightful place in a society and system that condemned them from the beginning.

After 20 years of formal education in America's "so called" educational institutions, I now realize how little I really knew. I was mis-educated about my history and culture. After being introduced to the teachings of the Nation of Islam I began to understand the importance of self-education and cultural pride. I am grateful for this experience because I'm now able to guide many Black men who still fall into the chasm of mental self destruction.

After "coming to my senses" I was inspired to teach African Americans about their glorious past achievements and the enormous possibilities for the future once they acquire an appreciation for their own culture.

2

Many are familiar with a process called *"Psychological Warfare."* This is a process where Black males are taught to psychologically hate themselves without ever realizing it. The most devastating effect of this mental crime is that the cycle is repeated for subsequent generations.

African-Americans must understand that, as the rest of the world slept in utter ignorance, our people were self-taught scholars. The remaining cultures marveled at our ingenuity and begged to learn from us.

May this information serve as motivation for Black men to critically assess where they are at this point in their lives. May they use this information to empower others. This process is essential for Black men and women to create a more positive life for our youth, families and community.

Remember **"Faith in God"** and "**Knowledge of Self**" are the building blocks for self-love.

"I'm sick and tired of being sick and tired."
–Fannie Lou Hamer

CHAPTER TWO

Our children are the future. Invest in them now.

THIRTY THINGS TO KNOW ABOUT RAISING BLACK BOYS

Thirty Things to Know About Raising Black Boys

1. Instill a healthy respect and devotion for God in all boys.

2. Teach them the value of daily prayer.

3. Administer discipline, and teach responsibility and values to your sons. Give them chores like cleaning their rooms, taking out the trash, mopping, sweeping, cutting the neighbor's grass or have them volunteer for a local community-based organization. Program their time and make sure they always have something to do. If you run out of physical activities for them, give them book reports to complete at home and have them present oral reports to you and the family. "An idle mind is the devil's workshop."

4. Teach them manners and respect. Demand that they say "yes sir, no sir, yes ma'am, and no ma'am." Make sure they say "thank you" when somebody gives them something.

5. Teach them their history starting with the Great Kings and Queens of Africa. Move on to the slave trade and discuss its relevance to present day activities.

6. Give them a sense of direction relative to goals that you have set for them.

7. Teach them self-respect along with respect for others. Teach them not to compromise their values or spiritual beliefs for anyone.

8. Teach them conflict resolution and the proper way to handle conflict when it arises.

9. Encourage sports participation. It builds collaborative relationships with peers along with increasing "mental toughness."

10. Teach them to be neat, orderly and to take pride in their personal appearance.

11. Show them how to excel in school and to strive for excellence and not to settle for mediocrity. Let them know that getting good grades in school does not make them a "punk, sissy or nerd." Remind them that the "nerds" (smart children with good grades) are the ones who will actually run the world.

12. Take pride in being a role model for your child. Be disappointed if he claims anybody other than mama and daddy as his number one role models.

13. Teach your sons the difference between needs and wants. Example: Your son has one hundred dollars. He **wants** a $100.00 pair of tennis shoes. But he **needs** to pay his car insurance which also costs $100.00. Teach him to do the responsible thing.

14. Parents should always lead by example.

15. Parents should be consistent with discipline, establishing rules, consequences, boundaries and setting limitations with children.

16. Parents should have some idea about the type of friends with whom their children associate. Parents should maintain open communication with the parent of the visiting child. Know something about your son's peers and their families.

17. If you're fortunate enough to have a car, use drive time to discuss issues that are critical to your child's development. Use the community and local events as a starting point to raise the awareness of your child. Turn off the car radio.

18. Establish a merit system where children earn the things they desire. Children will value these things more if they have to work for them. Children, like adults, don't place the same value on items that are handed to them on a "silver platter."

19.	Family time is important. Therefore make a point to sit down as a family and have a family dinner at least once a week. Use this opportunity to discuss critical issues regarding the child's development (example: College, community and social issues that affect our communities across the country.)

20.	Your home should be reflective of your culture. The home should be a showcase of the many achievements, struggles and triumphs that African Americans have demonstrated throughout their sojourn in the world. You should have a library of books in your house, especially books on Black culture and the many Black people who died so others might be able to read, write and enjoy the many social liberties that many of us take for granted.

21.	Teach your sons how to cook, sew, prepare meals, wash clothes, be self-sufficient and work for what they want. Teach them that household duties are not exclusive to women. Teach them to take pride in preparing meals for the family. Sign them up for cooking classes.

22.   Teach them the value of getting a good education and that education is not limited to the classroom. Give your sons homework, special projects and reading assignments in their spare time. Turn off the video and the "tell-lie-vision" if you want smarter, educated children. Let them know their education is sacred. Teach them that good grades follow them throughout life -- that personal and professional endeavors are measured by effort.

23.   Encourage your sons to watch the world news, local news and to read the daily newspaper. Teach them the importance of understanding world issues and how they "fit" in this world. Assign daily reports to them and solicit feedback.

24.   Teach your child good character, integrity and authenticity. There is no substitute for these virtues.

25.   Teach them that the world owes them nothing and that anything received in life usually comes about as a result of hard work and perseverance. Let them know that their goals are achievable and that their attitude often determines their "altitude" of success in life.

26. Teach them to volunteer their time, to donate money and lend resources to their respective communities and not to expect pay in return.

27. Teach them how to be a role model in their community and to take pride in being a good example for all people.

28. Teach Black boys the value of money and how to make money work for them. Teach them the importance of being an educated consumer and the value of being independent versus being dependent on other races of people for their goods and services. Teach them the value of being an entrepreneur, and a builder of their community.

29. Teach them how to buy a car, house, and other major purchase items. Teach them the many tricks that people use to enslave them if they are ignorant of business concepts. Teach them the discipline of saving money. Introduce them to the basics of stock markets, investments and other aspects of the economic world around them.

30. Teach them to enjoy life, have fun and to create a positive legacy. Be sure they understand that each generation's success is based upon today's work. Teach them to *"Learn and Return"* to their respective communities.

"A man's bread and butter is only insured when he works for it."
–Marcus Garvey

Birds teach birds how to fly. Fish teach fish how to swim. Black men must teach Black boys how to become responsible men.

THE BLACK MAN'S RESPONSIBILITY

The Black Man's Responsibility

1. Fish teach fish how to swim. Birds teach birds how to fly. Black men must teach Black boys how to become Black men. Black boys learn from their examples. The father should play a vital role in the child's development.

2. Many Black boys desire to be like their fathers. If the father has a positive self image and lives his life as a positive example, it is easy for the son to emulate the ways of the father. If the father is absent for whatever reason, it becomes customary for the son to follow the ways of the world.

3. Black men must be and become the vanguard for their community. This is necessary to eradicate the invading forces that dismantle the fabric of the community. They must stop the liquor merchants, foreigners and anyone else who moves into the community disguised as "benevolent" entrepreneurs who take valuable resources out of the community.

4. Black men must become father figures in the lives of Black boys who have no father present. The more Black boys see positive Black men demonstrating acts of kindness, caring, nurturing, and giving to their communities, the more likely they are to practice the same behavior.

5.   Black men must become builders of the community in which they live. It is paramount and prudent that Black boys participate in these activities in order to build self confidence. When Black boys see White men building skyscrapers, houses and businesses,   they have to wonder what their place is and if they're capable of doing the same.

6.   Black men must be proud, responsible and willing to sacrifice for future generations so that Black boys may have a better life. Black men must continue to overcome illiteracy in order to combat the social forces that plague them daily.

7.   Black men must be loving, positive and supportive of their daughters.   They must be shining examples for their daughters so that they might help them see what a positive Black man looks like and know how he should behave.

8.   Black men must set aside their religious differences and not be limited by religious affiliations. They must understand that "**We Are Our Brothers Keeper**" and that all Black men are socially obligated to be "**Elders of the Village**" in which they reside.

9.   Black men must be faithful, honest, God-fearing, supportive, and financially stable before seeking a wife. He must be loving to his wife who deserves a responsible mate.

10. Black men must communicate and share their feelings with their wives. They must seek positive counsel from those in the community who have demonstrated positive worth. Black men must learn to express their fears and correct their shortcomings so that they may become "whole" and be at peace with themselves.

"An ounce of example is more valuable than a ton of advice."
−Titus 2: 6-7

Real Black men are responsible, loving fathers who spend quality time with their children.

REAL BLACK MEN

"Real" Black Men

1. Real Black men are God-fearing and put God first and foremost in their lives.

2. Real Black men don't mind sharing their feelings.

3. Real Black men understand that it's okay to cry.

4. Real Black men will sacrifice for the good of their race.

5. Real Black men protect, maintain and provide for their families.

6. Real Black men spend time with young boys while helping to provide a positive male image in the absence of their biological fathers.

7. Real Black men are loving fathers to their children.

8. Real Black men spend time with their children.

9. Real Black men are responsible. They address their problems and work to solve them.

10. Real Black men don't physically or mentally abuse their wives, women or children.

11. Real Black men are gainfully employed and don't mind working hard to support their families.

12. Real Black men will die for a principle if it will benefit others.

13. Real Black men seek to elevate, empower, inspire and motivate their soul mate.

14. Real Black men take pride in marrying and being faithful to one wife or woman instead of practicing the playboy lifestyle.

15. Real Black men take pride in their history, culture and heritage.

16. Real Black men take pride in being a Black man.

17. Real Black men mean what they say, and say what they mean.

18. Real Black men take pride in building their own communities instead of watching others build it for them.

19. Real Black men take control of their own destiny rather than allowing others to control and determine their destiny.

20. Real Black men take pride in maintaining order and peace in their family, neighborhood and communities.

21. Real Black men aren't afraid to marry a woman who already has children.

22. Real Black men are intelligent. They value education and strive for excellence.

23. Real Black men marry within their race.

24. Real Black men are able to except their failures, build on them and use them as a source of motivation to effectively handle greater challenges.

25. Real Black men strive to create, maintain and sustain an economic base in their communities and encourage others to do the same.

"The mere imparting of information is not education. Above all things, the effort must result in making a man think and do for himself."

–Dr. Carter G. Woodson

CHAPTER FIVE

*Black boys grow up
with a sense
of rage and resentment
when their fathers
are absent
from their households.*

WHERE ARE YOU DADDY?

Where Are You Daddy?

Black boys in today's society are hurting because of the absent father. I have talked with countless young boys who yearn for their fathers or a strong Black man who will give them a sense of direction in life. The abandoned Black boy grows up with a misguided perception of manhood. Many are taught at an early age that they must assume the role of "the man of the house." This is confusing to young boys because they don't understand what manhood is all about.

Black boys don't know how to act or respond when they are questioned about their absent fathers. Many say, "it doesn't matter to me that he's not in my life." When boys make statements like this, they're disguising their true feelings. Every young boy desires to have a relationship with his father. When the father is absent, young boys internalize a sense of abandonment, rage and anxiety especially if their peers are fortunate enough to have a visible father in their lives.

Black boys tend to emulate other males in the community whether they be positive or negative. Sadly, the negative Black males in the community tend to have a greater influence on the younger Black males' behavior.

This happens because of the unwillingness of successful Black men to "mentor" fatherless boys. This void opens the door for a gang leader or drug dealer to become the idol in the life of a young Black male. So often this cycle of social destruction becomes the *"rite of passage"* for Black youth.

This chapter articulates the pain that young boys feel while growing up in a family where the father is absent due to incarceration, early death, divorce or abandonment. These early experiences often prove to be a major drawback in the lives of young Black males who are developing a level of sensitivity toward others. Many Black males feel a sense of rejection, shame and guilt about their absent fathers.

These early experiences, if not dealt with properly, have proven detrimental in the lives of young Black males. All too often, Black males experience similar situations of this type involving their absent fathers. They feel resentment, bitterness and jealousy toward Black males who do have responsible fathers in their lives.

The problem of the missing father is further compounded when young Black males grow up in a society that fears and misunderstands them and their rage. This misdirected energy finds itself in the classroom and other organized structures. Many males resort to drug abuse and gang involvement which eventually lands him in a juvenile facility or jail.

Financial and economic hardship contribute to the "disappearing act" of the Black father. Some men abandon the family because they lack resources to adequately care for them. This has proven to be a major stumbling block for Black men. In spite of all of these perils, many struggle to remain a vital entity in their households.

Black men must understand that regardless of financial constraints, limitations and their inability to provide for the family, they must "stick it out" if they want to have loving children who respect them as role models and parents. There can be no excuses for running out on the family. *Where **are** you daddy?*

"We must reinforce argument with results."
--Booker T. Washington

CHAPTER SIX

*"The ruin of
a nation begins
in the home
of its people."*

Ashanti proverb

SINGLE PARENT HOUSEHOLDS

Single Parent Households

Single parenting has reached epidemic proportions in today's nation. It is a tragedy that so many of our youth grow up in households without fathers. New research suggests that 70% of Black families are now headed by a single parent, usually the mother. The advantages of growing up in a dual parent household far outweigh that of single parent households. In many instances, the mother is left to rear the children singlehandedly, giving personal guidance and meeting the needs of the family financially.

This is an awesome responsibility for women personally, socially, financially and physically. Many times their sons grow up with a sense of shame, hurt, resentment and anger associated with their father's absence. When questioned about the absence of his father, the Black boy's response is a reaction of numbness or "who cares?" The ever-lingering issue of the father's absence becomes his source of rage which is acted out daily in schools across America.

The drawback or ripple effect of single-parent households leaves young Black males interpreting this experience as "the norm." This leaves women in a state of desperation and confusion. It sometimes causes Black women to turn to other women for sexual, personal and social gratification.

20

The single parent household, where fathers neglect their children, fail to pay child support or serve any kind of meaningful purpose in the lives of young males, has produced a generation of cold, callous Black males that has little regard for life itself.

When irresponsible Black men are questioned about their responsibility toward their children, the familiar response is: "*The White man got all the jobs and won't let me be a father to my children.*" As a Black man who sees the hurt, pain and disillusionment suffered by Black youth at the absence of their fathers, I say boldly, "**Shame, shame, shame on you.**" There can be **no** excuses when it comes to raising Black boys to be men. Regardless of the circumstances and conditions of the family, the Black man cannot continue to dodge his innate duty of responsible parenting to his children without serious repercussions.

Out of desperation, some Black mothers feel they have to take any man they can get. The result of this critical union is usually more illegitimate children, with no responsible fathers to rear them.

When some single mothers lack adequate finances, they settle for the next available "*irresponsible*" Black male for financial support. So often he comes to her with a whirlwind of promises of how he will be different from the last Black male in her life.

Single parent households also take on a different "twist" when there is a responsible Black male that assumes the role of the absent biological father. Although he dignifies the situation by marrying the Black mother, he may experience turbulence due to the Black mothers' history of poor relationships with men. Other problems can develop in the newfound union such as disciplinary issues, financial woes, and social discord.

The social and psychological experiences that the mother endured from previous relationships can be monumental. It is a challenge for the sustenance of the new relationship.

Conscious Black men salute Black mothers for their extraordinary ability to be "mother and father" to their children. This is a testament to the Black woman's fortitude, incredible perseverance and faith in God. Her internal fortitude has withstood the test of time to produce many great men and women.

"When elephants fight, it is the grass that suffers."
–Kikuyu Proverb

The mother's role in the upbringing of the male child is critical to his relationship with females. Her image and teachings influence the way he sees the world.

Maria Sampson
A.A.A.R.M.
Parent

BLACK MOTHERS

Black Mothers

There are many Black parents who perform a magnificent task of raising their children to be competent and productive members of society. The job of responsible parenting is critical to the success of Black youth. The old saying that "the apple doesn't fall far from the tree" is relative to the child's upbringing and the world's view of that child.

In this age where violence and negligence run rampant in the lives of Black youth, the Black mother often bears the blame for this dysfunction. Jawanza Kunjufu, author of **"Countering the Conspiracy to Destroy Black Boys,"** reports that Black mothers willingly raise their daughters to be self-sufficient, responsible and domesticated, while spoiling their sons. This destroys the opportunity for boys to develop independence and character.

Black mothers become overwhelmed by economic conditions when left alone to raise the children. There is a misconception about Black mothers which says they don't care about their children, and they shift the responsibility on others to raise them. However, there is no theory to support this claim. Child neglect is not exclusive to Black women. Most Black mothers love their children deeply and struggle to give them the very best.

One of our nation's leaders, the Honorable Elijah Muhammad said that the Black woman was the "mother of civilization" and that her role of parenting was crucial to the sanctity of nationhood. He added that the Black woman is her child's first teacher, nurse, doctor, and the foundation of the child's universe. The positive Black mother can be a conscientious influence on her children. She can encourage them to become high achievers and successful adults. However, it is necessary for the mother to seek self improvement along the way.

Children who have no guidance are often referred to as "little monsters" (one causing mischief and wreaking havoc). These children are viewed as a reflection of their parents. Generally, when you find a child with poor behavior, you're looking at a mirrored image of the parent. Our Black children are labeled misguided and "BAD" because they lack proper home training and discipline. These are some of the primary duties of the father. Once these basic responsibilities are met, the father and the mother can work toward instilling cultural pride and a sense of direction in the child.

In today's society it appears that Black males have forgotten their history lesson. There is an adage that says, "*those who fail to learn the lessons of history are doomed to repeat the same mistakes time and time again.*" Children are misguided today because their parents have not prepared them to handle the challenges of adulthood.

24

If parents seek to raise responsible children, they must understand their concise roles in child rearing. Parenting is one the greatest professions in the world. Every Black mother must realize that she is the chief architect in the development of her children.

It is paramount that Black mothers examine the parenting styles of their grandmothers. We must not continue to copy the Euro-centric style of child rearing. We must instill discipline in our children as well as our own set of spiritual beliefs, and moral values if we expect to see a change.

"We, the Black women of today, must accept the full weight of a legacy wrought in blood by our mothers in chains. As heirs of a tradition of perseverance and heroic resistance, we must take our place wherever our people are forging toward freedom."
–Angela Davis

CHAPTER EIGHT

Black men should be role models for their children. Black youth often emulate their father's actions. The presence of the father is critical to the child's development.

BLACK FATHERS

Black Fathers

Every Black boy is entitled to a personal relationship with his father. He should have a father who is a role model and a guide. A child should never put a sports figure like Michael Jordan, Charles Barkley or Penny Hardaway before his father. This question is often asked of youth: Whom do you want to be like when you grow up? The familiar response is usually a sports figure or with someone whom the child has no real relationship.

The sports figure that the child emulates could be a poor role model because of their character. A compelling role model is visible to the youth and their contributions are not merely monetary.

Black children who grow up without a father in the home experience a sense of anxiety. If the father is absent from the home, yet takes a positive and pro-active role in the child's daily life, he can still bridge the gap.

The absent father's actions have a boomerang effect on the entire family. Boys grow up with a sense of fury and frustration because there's no positive male to emulate. When boys feel abandoned, they become resentful. They don't understand why this "abandonment" happened to them. Girls, on the other hand, internalize their feelings. They may hold a grudge against all men because they fear that the man they marry will behave the same way as their father. Girls who have poor experiences with their fathers often view the Black man as irresponsible and of "no good."

The role of the Black father is critical to the survival and development of Black male children. Some responsible Black men not only care for their biological children, but mentor fatherless children as well.

The Black father has to accept the ultimate responsibility of being the man of the house, provider and the responsible party that ensures the success of the family. Our children are confused because the Black man has neglected his responsibilities of being a "real" man, provider and head of his household.

This has resulted in Black boys desperately seeking manhood – sometimes at the expense of taking the life of another Black male so that they may be considered "tough."

In recent years, the Black man has not acted responsibly. He has created a sense of resentment among Black boys who desire to be like their fathers when they reach adulthood.

It is painful when Black men talk about how bad our children are, while refusing to get involved in their lives in any meaningful capacity. The Black man has been psychologically damaged by a society that fears and degrades him. This accounts for some of the apathy and confusion felt by the Black man.

Most men gauge their manhood by the contents of their wallets. When the Black man in America has been systematically shut out of the financial market, it magnifies low self-esteem which results in family friction.

However, these hurdles do not excuse the countless number of Black men who are downright shiftless, lazy, pathetic, and good for nothing. These pitiful "excuses for men" only blab about the negative conditions facing the Black community while contributing absolutely nothing.

In the animal kingdom, the male species is the dominant one. He is the protector and provider of his family and community. The Black man in America could benefit greatly by adopting its habits and principles.

In order for the Black man to be a positive example to his children, he must seek self improvement first. If he lacks direction, he must revert to the practices of his forefathers.

"A man who won't die for something is not fit to live." – Dr. Martin Luther King Jr.

CHAPTER NINE

*"We are living
in a world
where your color
matters more
than your character."*

Sister Souljah

It's a Black "Thang"-- You Wouldn't Understand

A vast number of White Americans find favor with upwardly mobile African-Americans. However, there are stipulations regarding this favor. If controversy arises over a "heated or racial issue," these White Americans often reveal their true prejudice against all Blacks. Scenes often repeated in the ghettos of America depict an angry White police officer seeking to kill any Black youth. This is not a fantasy of prime time television. It is a reality for Black males living in America. So often, the Negro who strives hard to be an American forgets his history until he witnesses an incident similar to the Rodney King beating.

Many White folks are comfortable with the Negro whom they deem responsible and predictable. This receptiveness is focused at the lower-class Negro in the ghetto as well as the so-called upper class Negro who strives hard to fit into mainstream America.

For years, White America has been suspicious of any Black man desiring the best out of life. This Black man, in many White circles, is conveniently called the "uppity nigger."

This type of man presents a professional challenge because the White power structure views him as a threat to all who scurry up the corporate ladder. He is feared because his abilities may someday place him in a position that controls the American job market for Whites.

The point of this issue is that when Black males assemble to discuss pertinent issues relative to the empowerment of the African-American community, White racists get nervous. They look at this association as a form of betrayal, rebellion and militancy. Black males who campaign against racism and work to empower their communities are viewed as "un-American" especially if the subject relates to the abuse endured by the Black community.

Most liberal Whites think in terms of the human race and humanism. When topics arise concerning Blacks and the White power structure, the tables are turned. The views of many Whites remain the same regardless of the culturally diverse information that is offered them.

I'm reminded of a friend who teaches an Afro-American history course at a local college. She told me that liberal Whites who sign up for her class often drop the course before the semester is complete. She reports that in her twelve years of experience, no White male has ever completed the course.

31

The facts and statistics support the theory that many Whites are catatonic racists.   Given the power, wealth, resources, weaponry and military dominance by the White race, it's easy to see why they feel superior.

Many Whites who read this will find great comfort in dismissing the messenger while ignoring the message. An old Native American adage suggests that "one should not criticize another until he has walked a mile in his moccasins. " The message here is that Whites who read this may pronounce the messenger a radical Black militant who hates White Americans. Whites may say that Blacks are always "crying the blues" about their condition. They may say we do nothing to help ourselves.   This is false. Many Blacks work harder than Whites but suffer more economically. Financially speaking, Blacks are still at the "bottom of the ranks".

This may be hard for many Whites to comprehend. *After all it's a Black "thang," you wouldn't understand!*

CHAPTER TEN

"You may write me down in history
With your bitter, twisted lies,
You may trod me in the very dirt
But still, like dust, I'll rise."

Maya Angelou

THE BLACKER THE BERRY...

The Blacker the Berry . . .

The idea of having a discussion about interracial marriage may be appealing to some while offensive to others. There are people who feel uncomfortable about race relations, particularly where it relates to Black men and their relationships with White women.

Before I begin, I want to acknowledge the existence of successful Black men who are loving fathers and good husbands to their beautiful Black wives. Some of these men also take the time to serve as role models for their community. These men should be commended for having the strength to stay within their race while supporting Black women who are deserving.

When Black men marry outside of their race, it shortens the list of eligible men for single Black women. Black boys are desperately seeking fathers and role models. When Black men abandon their households and community it sends a poor message to their offspring.

For 400 years the Black man was enslaved psychologically and physically. He was brainwashed into believing that the White woman was the nectar of the world, yet was off limits to him. Because of this biased teaching, the White woman became more desirable to the slave. Remember the old adage that says, "you always want what you can't have?"

The Black man started believing that "landing" a White woman was the ultimate achievement in life.

More and more, we see a population of successful, professional Black men turning to White women for marriage and relationships. This raises the question, "What's wrong with Black women?" Why are so many financially stable Black men finding themselves in the arms of White women? Why can't Black men seem to find suitable Black women to marry? Seventy percent of Black families are headed by single mothers who are ready, willing, and eligible for marriage. These families desperately need a responsible Black man in the home.

Some say that love transcends color and that a person should not be prejudged by their appearance and skin color. Throughout this book, you will read about the horror of racial prejudice and how Blacks are still judged by the color of their skin. To further illustrate this fact, I'm pointing out the double discrimination against the Black woman who has been the backbone of this society for many, many years. In a perfect world, all people would be judged by their character and not by the color of their skin. One of the biggest problems with this is that we live in America – which means that we are a long way from racial harmony.

The intelligence of Black men will always be questioned by Whites. Even the most polished Black man has to prove himself in order to be accepted.

This places him under an infinite microscope. When he gets frustrated by this racial offense, Whites dismiss him as an "angry Black man."

When I look at other races of people, the men seem to be so content with marrying a woman who shares his ethnic origin. Many of them never even consider the possibility of marrying outside of their race. It seems that the Black man in America has been systematically trained to hate himself and those who look like him, which makes it easy for him to marry outside of his race.

I believe that God the Almighty blessed the Black man like no other. When you look at Black women you see one of the most beautiful creatures on the planet. God gave the Black man a beautiful woman who possesses every color hue on the spectrum. Black women's complexions come in shades of dark chocolate, caramel, raspberry, strawberry, peach, vanilla, light, bright and damn near white. It's like having a bountiful fruit basket filled with apples, cantaloupes, peaches, pears, grapes, watermelons, and bananas topped with a honey dew melon. The image of the Black woman makes your mouth water, just reading about her. On the other hand, when you look at White women, they just come in one shade -- nothing more and nothing less. This particular fruit basket has a limited selection. It's like having an apple or an orange with no other choices.

These fruits are good but variety is the spice of life – which further reiterates the point that Black men do not have to seek out White women for the sake of experiencing a change of color. He can stay at home and sample the best of all nectars in his fruit basket.

I personally love Black women and I believe that it is as natural as breathing to stay home and love, support and cherish the sovereignty of the Black woman.

Interracial marriages? I think not!

*Black women are
the most beautiful
of all the women
in the world.*

"Bridge over troubled waters."

Ebony and Ivory
Dollars and "Sense"

Let's start by saying there are exceptions to every rule. Now, welcome to the world of controversy. Aside from interracial relationships, there are few topics that unnerve people like Black wealth handed over to the "other side." Studies and observations show that a disproportionate number of Black professional athletes and entertainers date and marry outside of their race. We live in an age where many people (mostly the younger generation) say that color doesn't matter. Well, it must matter because Black women are seldom chosen as the spouse of a well-to-do Black professional and certainly not a well-to-do White professional. Why are White women so accessible to rich Black men? Aren't these the same women who would cringe at the thought of marrying a Black man if he were poor? Perhaps it's the social circle of professional men in which White women strategically entangle themselves. Why don't Black women prowl around after these men in the same manner? Or do they? If Black women are successful at getting their names on the "guest lists" at backyard pool parties or at "shoulder-rubbing" cocktail socials, why aren't they being wooed by wealthy Black and White men alike? And furthermore, why aren't they locking arms with these men at the wedding chapel?

Larry Davis, author of Black and Single reports that Blacks have the lowest interracial marriage rate of any nonwhite group. However, when Blacks do choose to marry outside of their race, Davis reports that the Black man is three times as likely to marry or date outside of his race than the Black woman. The numbers also change when you're addressing the wealthy Black man and his choice of a matrimonial partner. Most often, he chooses a White bride. There appears to be a great disparity with wealth among the races especially as it relates to the Black man's bank account and his willingness to share it with a White woman.

Those who say that love transcends color may want to take the following observations into consideration:

*   **High income Black Men:** tend to marry both high income Black and White women, low income White women, but seldom marry a low income Black woman.

*   **High income Black Women**: tend to marry both high income Black and White men, yet seldom marry low income White men or Black men.

*   **Low income Black Men**: tend to marry both low income Black and White women.

*   **Low income Black Women**: tend to marry low income Black men. However, trends show that this woman will accept the company and financial support of a White man who shares her same income bracket. The reason for this relationship could lie in the absence of the Black man.

*   **High income White Men**: as a whole, tend to marry White women <u>exclusively.</u>

*   **High income White Women**: tend to marry high income White men only. They may entertain the company of an upper-middle-income producing man but it is unlikely that he will be Black – unless his finances are really promising. The chances of a poor Black man "hooking up" with a wealthy White woman are slim. However, he may be allowed to drive "Miss Daisy."

*   **Low income White Men:** tend to marry low income White women, yet this man may date a Black woman who shares his same income bracket.

*   **Low income White Women**: tend to marry both low income Black and White men.

39

A closer look at these findings shows Whites with money, power and prestige almost exclusively marry within their own race. When White superstar athletes, businessmen and other professionals marry within their race the resources of that union benefit their families and respective community. The likelihood of Black superstar athletes (and their financial equals) marrying outside of their race is great. This partnership takes resources out of the Black community and hands it "over the fence." White families that benefit from this type of "inherited" money seldom appropriate dollars to help the Black community.

Blacks who marry Whites often say love is color blind. However, it takes an honest and intuitive person to admit that, in America, color does matter. And if race is not an issue, why is the marriage scale so imbalanced when it comes to Black male millionaires who seemingly set out to marry a White woman. One Black famous actor was quoted as saying, "I think I'll try something different – maybe an Asian or a Hispanic." One would think he was pondering over an ice cream selection. But if you take a look inside his money clip he has the option of choosing Vanilla if that's what his heart desires.

There seems to be an unwritten code of silence by upperclass Whites to always marry within their race and to keep the money, wealth and resources within their communities.

Maybe love isn't color blind. Maybe it has a problem with tinted shades. Because the average (working) Black woman doesn't stand much of a chance of marrying an oil tycoon or multimillion dollar "ball player" (especially if her direct competition is White).

Some famous, wealthy **Black men who chose White women (or Asian women) as their brides:**

1. Michael Jackson
2. Charles Barkley
3. Quincy Jones
4. Sidney Poitier
5. Harry Belafonte
6. Billy Dee Williams
7. O.J. Simpson
8. "Prince"
9. Dennis Rodman
10. Cuba Gooding Jr.
11. Georg Stanford Brown
12. Karl Malone

This list indicates a partial sampling of celebrities who found suitable mates in White women. However, some of their highly publicized relationships ended in divorce, spouse abuse and tragedy. So why do Black men with "fat pockets" date and marry White women? Do they do it for publicity? Do they do it in order to gain acceptance from the "other side?" Or do they truly believe that beauty is skin-deep? Even though there have been numerous studies on interracial relationships, most of the findings are inconclusive. Most of us want to say those Black men and White women are just "hot" for one another with "jungle fever." Whatever the reasons, interracial love will always be a subject of controversy.

We certainly applaud Black men like Bill Cosby, Denzel Washington and Michael Jordan who, not only married Black women but continue to give generously to charities that support inner city youth and their communities.

"When you rob your own race, you rob yourself."
– Anonymous

CHAPTER TWELVE

"*You must structure
your world
so that you are
constantly reminded
of who you are.*"

Na'im Akbar

**FANTASTIC? NOPE.
"BLACKTASTIC?" YEAH!**

Fantastic? Nope. Blacktastic? Yeah!

There is an old saying that reads, *"sticks and stones will break my bones, but words will **never** hurt me."* This is so untrue. You may question the relevance of this quote as it relates to this topic. To explain, displaced Africans who live in America have internalized certain words, vocabulary and jargon which takes on negative connotations when used in the context of the African-American experience.

We hear mainstream Americans say, "I've been blackmailed, the stock market crashed on black Tuesday, or beware of the black cat that crosses your path." These quotes brings to mind all of the things that bring bad luck. And the common denominator is the word, "black." These expressions can be more debilitating to a race of people than any physical imposition. They have the potential to admonish the inherent desire of a people to be free by convincing them that the word "black" or anything associated with being Black is somehow negative.

This castigation is natural when you live in a country that suppresses the culture of another. The weaker culture often adopts the practices and ways of the dominant culture, especially if that minority group is "culture less." In the case of African-Americans, their culture was literally wiped out with the advent of slavery.

43

Our once-celebrated culture revered by all nations of the earth is now systematically being destroyed and made a mockery of by the very people who stole, erased, and even claimed aspects of it.

Your every action, governed by a mental thought process dictates what act will be demonstrated subsequently in your life. Therefore, if African-Americans are to ever gain the level of respect achieved by other races of people, it is imperative that they modify the existing vocabulary imposed upon them by White society. They must begin to create, redefine and establish words ("ebonics" excluded) that give rise to a race of people considered by many to be mentally deaf, dumb and blind to the art of vocabulary.

A friend introduced me to the idea of using the word "blacktastic." He spoke of other words that give "rise" to a race of people who are battered and oppressed by common language. We must remember that language has the ability to serve as a psychological tool that offers hope and inspiration.

When I'm asked how I feel, I respond by saying, "blacktastic." It is a positive response while using the word, "black" -- quite the opposite of "blackmail or blackball." It may sound awkward initially because we're not used to hearing the word "black" associated with anything positive.

As you begin to experiment with the word "black," using positive expressions, you may ascertain that you're developing a more positive approach to how you see yourself.

Sticks and stones will break my bones and words will clearly hurt me.

CHAPTER THIRTEEN

*"You cannot fix
what you
will not face."*

James Baldwin

Is It Too Black For You?

This chapter addresses Whites who claim **not** to be racist in their views toward people of color. The idea of a universal brotherhood where all people live as "one" is synonymous with America, baseball and apple pie. The ugly truth is that this concept vanishes when Black men seek employment to support their families. Many racists get "bent out of shape" when Blacks are hired for jobs that they believe were meant for them. There appears to be a baseline margin on what racist Whites believe Black males can do, what they can own and where their "place" ought to be.

There is a universal cry among Black men regardless of their social and economic status in America. This cry echoes the Black man's belief that America is partial to Whites where employment is concerned. Some might say that unemployed Black men are looking for an easy way out and don't really want to work. This is not true of all Black men.

It is easy to see the imbalance of employment in this country. Something is wrong with this picture. Where is democracy relative to employment? Shouldn't everyone have the same advancement opportunities in this society?

There will always be people like Supreme Court Justice Clarence Thomas, Ward Connerly, and Armstrong Williams. All of these men oppose affirmative action. These men will tell you that Black men should stop complaining and be happy with the crumbs that fall from the White man's table.

This Machiavellian ideology parallels the same thinking of the house slave and the field slave. The house slave always found a reason to love his master because of the slight advantage given him by his slave master – an advantage that the field slave didn't get. He was favored because of his servitude and obedience to his slave master, especially when it involved the "backstabbing" of the field slave.

Collectively, Black men are wary of Whites because of White socioeconomic power. Whites control the social systems that govern America. It is imperative that Blacks take an active stance against the economic oppression imposed upon them by White society.

Most Black people go to work everyday and do the best they can with what they have. The problem arises when Blacks expect to move up the "corporate ladder" yet are pulled down -- one rung at a time.

47

I don't anticipate that my White colleagues or the "Negro" community will accept these arguments, or even understand my point. They will probably argue that this is a racist viewpoint that Black males only complain about, but really doesn't exist.

"We realize that our future lies chiefly in our own hands. We know that neither institution nor friends can make a race stand unless it has strength in its own foundation; that races like individuals must stand or fall by their own merit; that to fully succeed they must practice the virtues of self-reliance, self respect, industry, perseverance and economy."
--Paul Robeson

CHAPTER FOURTEEN

"When the Negro learns what manner of man he is spiritually, he will wake up all over... He will rise in the majesty of his own soul. He will glorify the beauty of his own brown skin...and he will redeem his body and rescue his soul..."

Nannie Helen Burroughs

RACIAL SELF-HATRED: JOE BLOW IN THE GHETTO

Racial Self-Hatred:
Joe Blow in the Ghetto

This story is about a client who experienced chemical dependency, problems with racial identity and low-self-esteem. His problems are a reflection of those suffered by many Black men who lack personal direction, guidance and a cultural foundation. When treating clients, I often give them an evaluation to assess the existence of a cultural base. If these clients are more Americanized than Afrocentric, this indicates a major problem with their identity and culture. They usually have low self-esteem relative to being a responsible Black man. These are the four question posed to one client and his responses to them:

Who Am I?

" I'm a Black man trapped in the White world trying to maintain my sanity, my morals and good judgment in a society that has already determined that I will fail. I'm a Black man trying to stay sober in a society that feeds me drugs and makes me hate myself, my "brother" and disrespect my "sisters." I am a Black man that has contributed to my destruction and almost the annihilation of my own people. I am a Black man free, but still a slave to the ignorant mentality that has made me my own overseer. The psychological chains around my neck make sure that I never fall back into consciousness of who I really am."

What is My Mission and Purpose in Life?

My mission and purpose in life is to stay on the destructive path of evil and to do the devil's work, because I have no knowledge of who God is. I seek to destroy my family values, pollute my community with drugs and honor the words of my slave master. I vow to stay high and be a worthless "nigga" and worship money, drugs, women or anything else that makes me feel powerful. If any "nigga" don't like it, Im gonna "bust a cap in his a_s! See, I hate myself, so don't expect for me to show you no love. I know that being an ignorant "nigga" is an art that I have perfected. I'm trying to be the best "nigga" that I can.

What do I like about being Black?

I like nothing about being Black. My history-- I have very little knowledge of it. I see no pride or decency among my race. We poison each other for monetary gains and we take pleasure in genocide and annihilation of our own kind. We fear the White man as if he were a god and reject God as if he were a "nigga". We look at those who deliver God's message as insane fools. The only pride I take in being a Black man is seeing my people revert back to the spiritual and intellectual beings we were before we fell from grace. My people are like the children of Israel, stubborn and rebellious, setting themselves up for their own self-hatred and annihilation.

What is my reason for living?

My reason for living is to overcome the triggers of life and my drug addiction, to understand myself, my true worth and spirituality like all Black men who are trapped in a schizophrenic lifestyle. We don't know if we are good or bad, or Black or White. My reason for living is to tear down the wall that has stopped me from being a productive human being; the wall that society has placed around me in my our of unconsciousness. Now that I have gained the level of consciousness to write these words, I still feel as if I'm blind groping in darkness, ignorant, losing my consciousness as I write these words because very few of us see the light to break down the wall that has kept us in darkness and ignorance.

"We wear the mask that grins and lies."
--Paul Laurence Dunbar

CHAPTER FIFTEEN

*"Lord I may not be
what you want me to be
but I thank God
I'm not what
I used to be."*

WHERE'S JOE BLOW?

Where's Joe Blow?

The horrors of slavery were so devastating that it robbed this client of his identity, culture and heritage. He became so immersed in American culture that he lost the value system that was laid before him by his African ancestors. When a man is robbed of his native culture, language, religion, God and history, the effects often prove to be irreversible. This client is a victim of racial self-hatred where he has accepted America's indoctrination of self-annihilation and genocide against his own race. This question should be asked: Do all Black males use these trials as a reason to cause trouble in their communities? The harsh reality is that many Black males who fall victim to this type of mentality end up being a menace to their race, family and respective communities.

This client had to be "**transformed**" into a man who loves himself, his race and community. He had to undergo a rigorous indoctrination of his rich history and its cultural achievements in order to find self-worth. The infusion of Black cultural awareness often proves to be the missing ingredient for clients like "Joe Blow" to turn their lives around.

Additionally, these Black males require re-education and re-training (required elements at school and at home.) These tools are necessary for reactivating their "internal good." Black boys are not bad at birth. What they experience is learned behavior. They mimic their examples.

This client faced his drug addiction and now takes pride in being a Black man. He teaches young Black boys in the community about positive choices and lifestyles changes. After learning about his African culture, rich history and success of other African-Americans, this client became so inspired that he finished high school, college and medical school. It is pleasing to note that he has become a highly respected medical doctor in the United States.

"The bumblebee's wings are so thin and its body so big, it should not be able to fly. The only problem is, the bee doesn't know that."
--David Lindsey

" *A climate of alienation has a profound effect on the Black personality, particularly on the educated Black, who has the opportunity to see how the rest of the world regards him and his people. It often happens that the Black intellectual thus loses confidence in his own potential and that of his race. Often the effect is so crushing that some Blacks, having evidence to the contrary, still find it hard to accept the fact we really were the first to civilize the world.*"

Cheikh Anta Diop

BLACK EDUCATORS

Black Educators

It is satisfying to know that African Americans are furthering their education by pursuing masters' and doctorate degrees. Schooling requires self discipline and perseverance, therefore those seeking higher education must have a personal desire to achieve. We salute all who have achieved a higher level of proficiency in education.

Black educators who excel in education should have a personal obligation to be role models in the Black community. They should strive to preserve its heritage and work to improve its future.

Some Black educators who teach at the college level forget their cultural roots and the Black struggle. So many aspire to be part of an educational institution that resents their level of educational achievement.

Black men who are teachers, university professors and administrators are highly scrutinized when they apply for these positions. They are expected to be twice as qualified. Additionally, their "lingo" and attire cannot be as "laxed" as it may be for their White counterparts. These Black teachers, professors, and university officials internalize feelings of inferiority. They begin to feel frustration while seeking to find an acceptable place in these educational institutions.

Many Whites, as well as Blacks believe that Blacks who have reached high levels of educational proficiency have gotten there by chance or maybe even through "token" acceptance.

Some Black educators (male and female) have lost their allegiance to the Black community. Those who fall in this category have forgotten their roots. It is the duty of these educators to give something back because many are crying out for their help. It is not enough to walk around gallantly passing out business cards with every initial in the alphabet on it. What's impressive is getting back to the foundation on which you still stand.

Past Black educators built institutions with the future in mind. These institutions were meant to hire, guide and teach African Americans. Very few schools are managed by Blacks today. These Blacks are too busy struggling to "fit in" where they are. Unfortunately, the respect and influence they seek may never materialize.

"The Black Man Must Turn Inward. Let all Black scholars, scientists, preachers, teachers and leaders turn within to develop ourselves and our people so they may rise as a people."
-Minister Louis Farrakhan

The media often portrays Black males as criminals, comedians or "jocks." Fortunately, more Blacks are gracing the "airwaves" with critical feedback.

BLACK YOUTH AND THE MEDIA

Black Youth and the Media

Our Black youth have the potential to excel at any level they desire. America tries to convince us that our Black children are genetically inferior to their White counterparts. Perhaps, the greatest difference between the two races is the mind set that both races possess.

White children are expected to achieve, to be smart and succeed in a society that has provided many avenues to ensure their success. The majority of Black children are expected to fail. This "credit" is given to a system that exalts "white power" in everyday life. Everyone is influenced by the media. Therefore, if Whites are always depicted as the powerful forces in America, this belief is mentally reinforced.

Images that Blacks see on television and on the "big screen" that presumably reflect their lifestyles can be convincing as well. It is extremely harmful when Black youth pattern themselves after pimps, dope dealers, and "gang bangers." It's a travesty when the top box office movies for Blacks are "Boys in the Hood" and "Booty Call." Youth become brainwashed into believing that the portrayed characters are their heroes.

This psychological warfare hinders the self-esteem of young Black males and females. Psychology shows that the images you see most, ultimately become you. The media seems to take pleasure in exposing and stereotyping minorities in this country. This effort serves to further divide a racially troubled nation.

The effects of the media are so overwhelming that even the most conscious-minded African-American can be seduced by the scores of negative images. America appears to be on a downward course of self-destruction stemming from internal rot. This nation has reached a "fork in the road" where it either submits to the principles of freedom, justice and equality, or dies of greed and moral decay.

Our Black youth have been appointed the social outcasts in America. This belief is perpetuated by the White media. Our youth don't realize that they are systematically being led to the psychological slaughterhouse in America. Additionally, they are occupying incarceration facilities which only serve to destroy the minds and bodies of our youth. America's failing prison system has become the new plantation for Black males.

Black youths today appear to have little knowledge of their history and civil rights. They are ignorant of the sacrifices made by their ancestors which have awarded them the freedom and privileges that they take for granted.

Black males prey upon each other today because they don't see each other as brothers. The absence of their history and culture makes it easier for them to harm and destroy those individuals that look like them.

It is important to note that Black youth mimic their parents' actions as well. Our children are ignorant to their history and culture because their parents and role models lack knowledge of their history. The relevance here is that when a race of people knows it's history, culture and legacy, their interaction with one another is different. This interaction becomes one of mutual respect for community and history.

"If you have no confidence in self, you are twice defeated in the race of life. With confidence you have won even before you have started."
–Marcus Garvey

CHAPTER EIGHTEEN

"It is the fool
whose own tomatoes
are sold to him."

Akan proverb

MONKEY SEE - MONKEY DO

Monkey See - Monkey Do

"Monkey See - Monkey Do" confronts the great number of African-Americans who are inspired by fashion and "the moment." Sporting today's fashions and being caught up in the moment are temporary and useless comfort zones adopted by many. The only victor is the store merchant who becomes wealthier and wealthier at the expense of "Negroes" who seek validation from their peers as well as society according to how well they're dressed.

Blacks who try to impress others by simply looking good have earned the undisputed title as the "best looking, poor people" in the world.

Merchants in every ethnic group snicker at Negroes who spend more than 450 billion dollars per year buying goods and paying for services that hardly benefit their respective communities. When foreigners celebrate our ignorance, it is humiliating, dehumanizing and degrading.

In the above scenario, who should be ashamed? Is it the foreigner who just happens to be a merchant and welcomes the opportunity to cash in on a "gold mine" profit in the Black community, or is it the fool who strives diligently to patronize the very people who have little or no interest in supporting the Black community or its needs?

The fashion merchants make an enormous amount of money off of the Black communities. Blacks in America are big spenders in the clothing industry. They fail to realize that their dollars are only supporting the comfortable lifestyles of many foreigners in our country.

The new clothing designers like "Tommy Hilfiger, Nautica, and Guess" prey upon the gullible people who know little about consumerism. When Blacks in America reduce their net worth to zero by spending every dime they earn on clothing, they continue to submerge themselves deeper into poverty.

Many Black women have also denounced their standard of natural beauty by "buying into" White society's concept of beauty. Some Black women are dying their hair blonde, while others are struggling with "the relaxer of the week." They're trying to find the one product that will make their hair the straightest. Ironically, a large number of beauty supply stores in America are now owned by Asians. They've, once again found an avenue to make a fortune off of Blacks. Another big business for Asians in the Black neighborhoods (aside from the ever-popular Chinese food "joint") is the must-have nail salon. Black women are flocking to the Asians and Koreans for all of their beauty services. Have Black women forgotten that they are the most creative and innovative people in the world? Why allow these foreigners to supply your hair care needs? Why allow Asians to sell you hair-damaging chemicals when your hair is the strongest of any race of people?

In an effort to look as "un-African" as possible, some Black women have reverted to sporting blue, green and violet contacts in their eyes. Black women must realize that the Creator makes no mistakes. Black women are beautiful just the way they are.

Black women are not the only ones who are buying into fads. Our Black males are killing one another over designer clothes, popular tennis shoes and other so-called "gear." The idea of Black males seeking acceptance by wearing sagging designer pants, flashing fake gold teeth, and donning "Mr. T-like" chains around their necks is utterly ridiculous. It is imperative that we start teaching our brothers and sisters about the creativity that originated long before Liz Claiborne, Donna Karan, Polo and Tommy Hilfiger. Our African ancestors would be highly insulted by our "monkey-see, monkey-do" practice of life.

"The basic tenet of black consciousness is that the Black man must reject all value systems that seek to make him a foreigner in the country of his birth and reduce his basic human dignity."
–Steve Biko

CHAPTER NINETEEN

"Beware of false prophets,
who come to you in sheep's
clothing, but underneath
are ravenous wolves."

Matthew 7:15

BLACK PREACHERS

Black Preachers

Preacher or Pimp? Man or mouse? Friend or foe? Saint or sinner? Those who read this chapter may think the author is opposed to the preachers in the Black community. You may think that one who raises these questions is of ill repute. One may even assess that the author is against religious men who profess to be of God while serving the African-American community.

On the contrary, preachers and ministers who are "doers" of the Word deserve respect and appreciation unlike those who make a hearty living off of poor people who are seeking spiritual direction. The modern day preacher/pimp poses as the great emancipator waiting to bestow blessings from heaven above on the so-called heathens who are in search of a spiritually guided lifestyle.

Many preachers use a lot of dramatics while delivering the Holy Word. When the word, "Jesus" is presented in this fashion, some African-Americans respond so emotionally that they lose sight of reality in their church. African-Americans are most vulnerable and are willing to give monies to support some ministries that have proven "vision less" and counterproductive toward liberating the Black community. The most popular structure in the Black community appears to be a new church with a liquor store across the street from it.

The irony is that Black preachers often refuse to act boldly against liquor merchants, "crack" dealers and other intruders that violate the Black community.

Our misguided Black people will continue to support the preacher without using logic as long as his message is couched with the name of the "Holy Ghost" and "Jesus." I once visited a highly respected church in my local Black community and was hoping to gain more knowledge about the Gospel. Much to my dismay, the church members sang, shouted and music was played for approximately two hours before the preacher reached the podium. Upon his arrival, he spoke for nearly fifteen minutes. Ten of those minutes were spent chanting the word, "Jesus." But no real message was conveyed. I kept an open mind but I did not get the spiritual encouragement from this particular service.

After visiting the church, I was saddened because of the wasted potential in that Black church. These churches have the ability to empower the Black community, but are limited because of blind leadership. The buffoonery in some churches is shameful. Sunday morning services seem to be a continuation of the Saturday nightclubs throughout many Black communities. The pews are filled with members of the secret Saints' society who party all Saturday night, then flock to the church on Sunday morning looking to pray their guilt away.

The Black preacher who "talks loud and says nothing" is the one whom the White man loves the most because he presents no real threat to "the establishment." Whenever an incident arises, the Black preacher is used as a buffer to neutralize potentially explosive situations ignited by the White power structure.

On the contrary, I have seen outstanding Black leadership in other churches. Their leaders perform tremendous works in the African American community and improve the quality of life for its members. I respect preachers who truly understand God's Word as it relates to the empowerment and liberation of our people.

"From the fruit of his words a man has his fill of good things, and the work of his hands comes back to reward him." --Proverbs 12:14

CHAPTER TWENTY

"You've been tricked!
You've been had!
Hoodwinked!
Bamboozled!"

El-Hajj Malik El-Shabazz (Malcolm X)

The Case of the Negro

Webster's dictionary defines the word "Negro" as a member of the Black race. Renowned leader, Malcolm X defined Negro as something that is literally dead. Historically, the word was created in an effort to separate the African race from its homeland. People from Italy are called Italians. People from Europe are called Europeans. People from Asia are called Asians. So why are people from Africa called Negroes? The word Negroid is a descriptive word. This word does not give credence to a person's homeland.

The U.S. Constitution bears certain inalienable rights of being an American and living in this country. One of those rights is the right to empower yourself, community and family. It appears as though the horrors of slavery were so devastating that it caused the Negro in America to lose his mind and any responsibility toward trying to reclaim it. This point of view reveals that the Negro in America seems to be satisfied with anything that is handed to him. He can be called anything and given anything as long as it relates to the idea of being an American.

All of this means that the Negro in America talks about liberation while the great majority sit idly by while waiting for the White masses to liberate them. Elijah Muhammad, of the Nation of Islam, once said that the same man who would not treat you right, certainly would not teach you right.

Individual, as well as group effort, is required to make vital changes for our African race. However, some Black organizations fail. Why? Here's a partial list: complacency, irresponsibility, futile effort, disinterest, apathy, laziness, jealousy, destructive mentality, hatred and social discord. The passivity of the Negro in America is very real and consistent with his lack of progress. He has been brainwashed into accepting his "detached" title, "the Negro." This may be relative to his inability to commit to structured organizations. Could it be that because he was stripped of his homeland that he bears no sense of belonging? This may be a fact. But must he abide in this? No! He must learn to re-associate himself with the Motherland, Africa. He must somehow reflect his true belonging to a great continent, whether it is in the style of his clothing, the displaying of the natural hair, the artwork in his home, or even the name by which he is called.

How can a nation be built that will empower the family and community while the great majority of Negroes are unskilled, unaccountable, irresponsible and immersed in foolishness? How does a race emerge from the darkness while possessing the mind set of a cockroach that struggles to survive? Ruth Shay, a civil rights activist, once said that when you don't know that you have been spit upon, it doesn't matter what else you think that you know. The point is that we must open our eyes to our survival as a race.

Once upon a time the great Marcus Mosiah Garvey said, "Up You Mighty Race, You Can Accomplish What You Will." I wonder if he would still hold that point of view given the complacency of the Negro today.

"When you control a man's thinking, you do not have to worry about his actions. You do not have to tell him where to stand or to go yonder. He will find his "proper place" and will stay in it. You do not need to send him to the back door. He will go without being told. In fact, if there is no back door, he will cut one for his special benefit."
–Dr. Carter G. Woodson

CHAPTER TWENTY-ONE

"No person is your friend
who demands
your silence
or denies your
right to grow."

Alice Walker

Your Love for the Enemy

Revolution in America, in the universal and global sense of the word, will probably never happen. It is unlikely because major institutions govern America and keep it operating in an orderly fashion.

The American Negro strives hard in America to be an "American." This is a concept precious to White Americans who invaded this land. Blacks will never see the "promised land" because they have no ownership in the American system.

The notion of Blacks finally being accepted in America is unlikely. The saddest part about this is that Blacks are still struggling to validate their own self-worth as Americans. Few have taken the time to search their souls and examine their rich history. Exercising these two forms of freedom will initiate some degree of worthiness.

There are few who fully understand the psychological effects of a people who are seeking acceptance from a majority culture. It usually results in a spiraling maze of racial self-hatred and an inferiority complex. The hypocritical notion of living in a color blind society or a multiethnic society is unrealistic. America reminds the Negro every day that he's still a "nigger."

The White man works diligently to abolish any vehicle by which the former slave can pull himself up by his bootstraps. The White forefathers have stripped the ancestral culture from every dark race of people throughout history.

68

Reparations and affirmative action can be frightening experiences for the White man. He won't concede without a fight. The concept of leveling the playing field has been downplayed resulting in what many people refer to as "reverse racism."

We now have "Negroes" campaigning for their own demise. This premise stems from the days of Willie Lynch who devised a celebrated plan for controlling and maintaining slaves. His theory focused on the psychological means of sustaining slavery where the slave worked to maintain his own enslavement.

The American "Negro" will never rise up to slay his four hundred-year-old enemy because he hasn't been trained to do so. He's only been trained to hurt, harm and destroy those that look like him. He works ambitiously against other Blacks even when they are working toward the liberation of African-American people.

The "Negro" believes a benevolent White man, perhaps with flapping, white wings, will fly out of the sky one day and offer him paradise. This is the thinking of a slave. A slave loves the White man so much that he will discount the truth at all costs.

For 400 years Africans were taught to worship an image. This image was depicted as a White man with wavy blonde hair and blue eyes. They said his name was Jesus. This was the birth of psychological destruction for the mis-education of the African.

69

The process of mind control and learned helplessness was studied in the early 1800's when a social scientist conducted a study using dogs that were beaten repeatedly. They internalized a sense of learned helplessness.

The "Negro" has internalized the same principles and has mastered these principles to a degree of perfection. No other race of people in history has come close to accepting this type of psychological destruction.

Today's White man can sleep comfortably knowing that his former slave still holds the internal principles that were pummeled into his psyche more than 400 years ago.

Maybe this explains the reason why Negroes burn down their own property instead of the property of their enemy when they revolt against some injustice.

America would like to thank the "Negro" for his four hundred years of dedication and commitment to his continued enslavement.

CHAPTER TWENTY-TWO

*"You will never know
who you are
in the world
until you
know thyself."*

Dr. John Henry Clarke

HOW BLACK IS YOUR COFFEE?

How Black Is Your Coffee?

Now that I have your attention, the metaphor here simply refers to your commitment to the salvation of Black people. There is a segment of our community known for its continued effort in educating African American people in spite of the overwhelming misinformation imposed upon them by White society. Despite this tireless effort, many Negroes insist on being misled.

There is another segment of our community that appears reluctant to get involved in anything that's progressively Black. Their ambivalence stems from years of subconscious and psychological brainwashing which systematically makes them resentful toward people who are a reflection of them. This is a form of racial self-hatred.

America has conditioned Blacks to work toward their own destruction. This system reflects America's vulture-like mental destruction of a people.

The new age "cosmopolitan" Black person void of culture often expresses no allegiance to the Black community – only to America. This type of Black person is most dangerous because their physical (Black skin) appearance denotes one thing, while their "White mentality" indicates another.

71

There are also Blacks who have benefitted from the sacrifices made by the Black struggle, affirmative action and other legislation designed to balance the scales of racial injustice.

A great majority of our people find it convenient to be a member of the Black race at one time, yet, at other times, choose to denounce their racial heritage. So many Blacks are quick to claim "white blood" or Indian roots in their genealogical lineage. But if you mention the word African, they begin to stutter or blatantly deny having any connection with Africa. Most Negroes choose to be Black when they need the support of their race after a racial incident. This is the only instance where they will speak out on the abuse of the Black race.

It's despicable to find Negroes who prostitute themselves and the Black community while seeking favor, status or association with White society. Their goal is a lofty one that only yields dividends to the individual who's "selling out." How black *IS* your coffee?

"If there is no struggle, there is no progress."
--Frederick Douglas

AAARM is an organization designed to empower African-American youth to be positive and productive members of society.

What is A.A.A.R.M.?

A.A.A.R.M. is the acronym for the *Association of African-American Role Models*. This organization was founded June 1986. Its purpose is to help stem the tide of youth violence and to empower African-American youth to be positive and productive members of society.

A.A.A.R.M. has worked with approximately 15,000 African-American youths over the past 13 years providing mentors, academic tutoring, counseling, parent support group meetings, employment, resume writing, job fairs, scholarship assistance, college tours, overnight retreats, out-of-town trips, cultural forums, educational seminars and mental health related services. Other components of A.A.A.R.M. are as follows:

Mission Statement - To empower African-American youth to be positive and productive members of society.

Focus - Self-esteem, Self-Motivation, Self-Development and Cultural Enrichment.

Purpose - To expose minority, disadvantaged, and "at-risk" youth to positive African-American role models.

Income Level - Income levels are not a factor when participating in the A.A.A.R.M. program. The program is free of charge.

Ages - The general ages of the participants are 9 - 19. However, the program is not limited by age. No one is too young or too old to benefit from the many activities sponsored by A.A.A.R.M.

Gender - The program serves both males and females.

Location - A.A.A.R.M. meets every Thursday from 6:00 p.m. - 8:00 p.m. at Saint Louis University - Tegeler Hall, 3550 Lindell Blvd. It is located in midtown St. Louis.

Pertinent Information - We feel that youth everywhere are at risk. Today, many of our youth appear to be confused for numerous reasons. Part of the problem is a lack of positive guidance in the home and a breakdown in the family structure.

Rites of Passage Program - Youth undergo an eight-week manhood/womanhood training program designed to instill pride, responsibility, maturity and respect for personal growth and development. They receive a plaque, T-shirt and local recognition as honorary graduates of Phase I of the role model program upon completion. The program has four phases where youth mentors are trained to facilitate and coordinate A.A.A.R.M. programs.

Funding - The A.A.A.R.M. program is supported by the generous donations from the community, fund-raising activities, membership donations and state grants.

Goals of the Organization are as follows:

1.   To expose "at-risk" African-American youth to positive African-American role models.

2.   To emphasize the importance of academic development relative to career opportunities.

3.   To stress the belief that personal and career goals are obtainable through academic preparation.

4.   To empower African-American youth through information, education and cultural awareness relative to personal and community development.

"Men build institutions...so that four hundred years later their descendants can say, "That's what he left."
–Nai'm Akbar

"Train up the child in the way he should go and when he is old he will not depart from it."
                    Proverbs 6:22

INSPIRATIONS

Inspirations

Praise and honor are due to God the Almighty for making me the man I am today and for leading me to develop the *Association of African-American Role Models* organization. The Creator further blessed me in 1981. I met a counselor at Cardinal Ritter College Preparatory high school in St. Louis, Missouri. Verge "Sage" Gillam instilled a sense of pride in me. He taught me about dignity and gave me a sense of direction. He motivated many other students to achieve high levels of success.

He encouraged me to think for myself, to read and study from a Black perspective while making a difference in my community. He confronted many of my shallow beliefs about the Black man's responsibility. He challenged me to act like a man and do the right thing.

After reading the great history of the Black man, his achievements and struggle to overcome European domination, I became more inspired to become a role model and to make a difference in the Black communities throughout America.

I am eternally grateful to my uncle Calvin Perkins. He gave my brother and me the opportunity to work for Prosser's Moving (a storage company) every summer. While we worked, he taught us the value of a good education. Some days we moved furniture in the hot sun for ten hours. He always reminded us that without a good education, we could expect to work like this for the rest of our lives. Many times he "dished out" the discipline to us when we got "out of line." This was necessary for both of us to learn discipline, respect and responsibility.

Finally, I thank my mother for the many sacrifices, hardships and struggles she endured. She put all of her children in the right schools, and provided guidance. I'm thankful for all of the good deeds (too great to list) that she bestowed on our family during the difficult years. I thank God for her solid example, fortitude and unyielding desire to see her children succeed during the turbulent times which actually brought us closer together as a family.

"If we stand tall, it is because we stand on the backs of those who came before us."
-Yoruba Proverb

VI.

Final Word

from the

Holy Quran

Asr, or Time through the Ages.

In the name of Allah, Most Gracious, Most Merciful.

By (the Token of) Time (through the Ages),

Verily Man Is in loss,

Except such as have Faith,

And do righteous deeds,

And (join together)

In the mutual teaching

Of Truth, and of

Patience and Constancy.

Sura 103

VII.

Selected Bibliography

Akbar, N. 1984. *Chains and Images of Psychological Slavery.* Jersey City: New Mind Productions.

Davis, E. L. 1993. *Black and Single: Meeting and Choosing a Partner Who's Right For You.* The Ballantine Publishing Group. New York

Dubois, W.E. B. 1961. *Souls of Black Folk.* New York: Dodd, Mead & Co.

Farrakhan, L. 1979 -1996. *The Final Call.* Chicago, IL: Final Call Inc.

Jackson, J.G. 1970. *Stolen Legacy.* San Francisco: Julian Richardson Assoc.

Kunjufu, J. 1984. *Developing Positive Self-Images and Discipline in Black Children.* Chicago: African-American Images.

Muhammad, E. 1965. *Message to the Black Man.* Chicago: Muhammad Mosque of Islam, No.2

Thomas, P. & McDavis, R. *Black Men: An Endangered Species.* Journal of Counseling & Development. September 1987, p. 25.

Wilson, A. 1990. *Black -on-Black Violence: The Psycho dynamics of Black Self-Annihilation in Service of White Domination.* New York: Afrikan World InfoSystems.

Woodson, C.G. 1977. *The Miseducation of the Negro.* New York: AMS Press, Inc.

Wright, B. 1986. *The Psychopathic Racial Personality.* Chicago: Third World Press.

Understanding The
Crisis Of The Black Male

*A Handbook On Raising Black Boys To Be
Responsible Black Men*
by
Ajuma Muhammad

To order additional books, audio tapes or copies of the book
on Compact Disc, fill out the form below and mail to:

**Ajuma Muhammad
Providing Options
P.O. Box 78873
St. Louis, MO 63178
(314)768-2417/Office
(314)838-3096/Fax**

**Web Page address: www.aaarm.org
E-Mail address: amuha14223@aol.com**

	Order Form		**I want:**	
			( )# of Books	$10.00
			( )# of Tapes	$10.00
			( )# of CD's	$15.00
Name				
Address				
City State Zip				
Daytime Phone				Add $2.00 per item for Shipping & Handling
Total Enclosed:				
Thank you for your order.				